Girls' Health™

Breast Cancer Prevention

Paula Johanson

rosen publishing's
rosen central®

New York

Published in 2008 by The Rosen Publishing Group, Inc.
29 East 21st Street, New York, NY 10010

Library of Congress Cataloging-in-Publication Data

Johanson, Paula.
Breast cancer prevention / Paula Johanson.—1st ed.
    p. cm.—(Girls' health)
Includes bibliographical references and index.
ISBN-13: 978-1-4042-1947-2 (library binding)
ISBN-10: 1-4042-1947-1 (library binding)
1. Breast—Cancer—Prevention—Juvenile literature. 2. Breast—Care
and hygiene—Juvenile literature.
I. Title.
RC280.B8J62 2008
616.99'44905—dc22

                                                    2007005417

Manufactured in the United States of America

Contents

Introduction

Breast cancer is extremely rare in teenagers. It is very important to learn how to examine your breasts for what is normal for you and what may be an abnormality. In America, fewer than one in 20,000 women will be diagnosed with breast cancer before the age of twenty-five. This low risk is one that is best met by the personal choice of each person to examine her own breasts routinely, as well as having regular appointments with a doctor. If you get to know your breasts now and continue to be familiar with them as they grow and change throughout your life, you should be able to spot a problem early—and get help right away. Learning about breast cancer prevention is as important for your health as brushing your teeth or washing your hands.

1

Know
Your
Breasts

The breasts, or mammary glands, are milk-producing organs and a part of the woman's reproductive system. In contrast to the flawless breasts that people see on magazine models and movie stars, real-life bosoms come in a wide variety of shapes and sizes. Your breasts, like your face, are uniquely you. And, like much of the rest of you, your breasts will change throughout your lifetime. Some changes happen when you gain or lose weight, some as you grow older, and others if you become pregnant or breast-feed a baby.

It is your responsibility to get to know your own body so that you can keep it healthy. This means becoming familiar with the breasts you have, their cyclical changes, and individual development as you grow and mature. So what is natural or typical for you as far as your breasts are concerned? Believe it or not, most women have one breast that is slightly larger than the other. If the difference in size is one bra cup or more, you can

Breasts are one of the more visible symbols of femininity. When they first begin to develop, you may feel a mixture of pride, confusion, and fear. Developing breasts signify your entry into womanhood.

always buy the larger size bra and pad one of the cups to create a more balanced look.

The rate at which breasts grow varies from female to female, sometimes with one breast developing at a faster pace than the other. Many girls' breasts grow in spurts, and these growth spurts can keep on occurring into your late teens, twenties, and even your thirties.

Your breasts may look even or uneven in size until age sixteen or later. They may be noticeably budding as early as age eight or nine. They may be round, or pear- or teardrop-shaped. No two breasts are shaped the same way. Your genes will determine most of these factors. You inherit the genes for your basic breast shape. Your breasts may be similar to those of a family member at the same age, just like the color of your eyes or shape of your nose may be similar to that of a member of your family.

However, your body weight has a big influence on your bustline as well. If you gain extra body fat, your breasts will increase in size because about one-third of breast tissue is fat tissue. If you lose weight, your breasts will probably become smaller, too. Eating good, nutritious food throughout your life will not only help your body build strong bones and muscles, it will also help your breasts and other organs develop normally.

As your hormones change during your lifetime, your breasts may change, too. With pregnancy and aging, your breasts will probably get larger, fuller, and eventually more saggy. So whatever your breasts look like today, they are likely to look different next year and in the years to follow.

Nipples, like breasts, vary from person to person. Some women may have a bit of hair growing around the areola, which is the darker area surrounding the nipple. This is perfectly normal and

Unlike the perfect images seen in movies and magazines, real women's breasts come in all sizes and shapes— oftentimes with one larger than the other.

natural. The areola looks different in different women, varying widely in color and size. Fair-haired women typically have pinkish areolas, while those of dark-haired women and African Americans look brown or black. Nipples usually point away from each other, not straight ahead, as this creates the easiest access for a suckling baby cradled in a mother's arms. On older women, whose breasts have begun to sag, nipples may point downward as well. On men, nipples can vary, too.

Breast Self-Exams

Examining your breasts on a regular basis need not be a dull chore or a frightening task you do specifically to hunt for cancerous lumps. A breast self-exam, or BSE, can teach you about your body and its ongoing changes as you grow. Practicing a BSE can help you become more comfortable with yourself. Being comfortable with your body and your breasts might make you feel better about who you are.

As an adult, you may want to conduct a BSE every month, which is what most health experts recommend. As a teenager, however, this is probably not necessary. But it will be easier to remember if you practice your BSE on a regular basis, like a few days after your menstrual period ends. Maybe you will mark your calendar or journal to keep track of your menstrual periods and your BSE. You might even add a brief note if you buy a new bra with a larger cup size to help you track your body's changes.

If you are not sure how to examine your breasts or are not comfortable with it, you always can rely on a doctor to do the BSE for you. Once you've begun to develop breasts, each time you visit a gynecologist or your family physician for a regular checkup, he or she will examine your breasts for any abnormalities. It is unlikely that you or your doctor will find anything out of the ordinary, but it is always better to do regular checkups instead of ignoring little problems until they become big problems. Books, pamphlets, a nurse, or a doctor can help you learn to examine your breasts and tell you what you need to know about the most common—but harmless—breast problems.

The U.S. Department of Health and Human Services recommends the following method for a BSE:

1. Stand before a mirror. Inspect both breasts for anything unusual, such as any discharge from the nipples, puckering, dimpling, or scaling of the skin. (The next two steps are designed to

Do it yourself

Monthly breast self-exam

1 Stand before a mirror. Inspect both breasts for anything unusual, such as any discharge from the nipples, puckering, dimpling, or scaling of the skin.

The next two steps are designed to emphasize any change in the shape or contour of your breasts. You should be able to feel your chest muscles tighten while doing these steps.

2 Watching closely in the mirror, clasp hands behind your head and press hands forward.

3 Next, press hands firmly on hips and bow slightly toward your mirror as you pull your shoulders and elbows forward.

Some women do steps 4 and 5 in the shower. Fingers glide over soapy skin, making it easy to concentrate on the texture underneath.

4 Raise your left arm. Use three or four fingers of your right hand to explore your left breast firmly, carefully, and thoroughly. Beginning at the outer edge, press the flat part of your fingers in small circles, moving the circles slowly around the breast. Gradually work toward the nipple. Be sure to cover the entire breast. Pay special attention to the area between the breast and the armpit, including the armpit itself. Feel for any unusual lump or mass under the skin. Repeat the exam on your right breast.

5 Gently squeeze each nipple and look for a discharge.

6 Steps 4 and 5 should be repeated lying down. Lie flat on your back, right arm over your head and a pillow or folded towel under your left shoulder. This position flattens the breast and makes it easier to examine. Use the same circular motion described earlier. Repeat on your right breast.

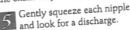

Although breast cancer is extremely rare in teenagers, it is very important to learn how to examine your breasts for what is normal for you and what may be an abnormality. Follow these steps for a breast self-exam.

emphasize any change in the shape or contour of your breasts. As you do these exercises, you should be able to feel your chest muscles tighten.)

2. Watching closely in the mirror, clasp your hands behind your head and press hands forward.

3. Next, press your hands firmly on your hips and bow slightly toward the mirror as you pull your shoulders and elbows forward. (Some women do the next part of the exam in the shower. Fingers glide over soapy skin, making it easy to concentrate on the texture underneath.)

4. Raise your left arm. Use three or four fingers of your right hand to explore your left breast firmly, carefully, and thoroughly. Beginning at the outer edge of the breast, press the flat part of your fingers in small circles, moving the circles slowly around the breast. Gradually work toward the nipple. Be sure to cover the entire breast. Pay special attention to the area between the breast and the armpit, including the armpit itself. Feel for any unusual lump or mass under the skin.

5. Gently squeeze the nipple and look for discharge. Repeat the exam on your right breast. Steps 4 and 5 should be repeated lying down. Lie flat on your back, left arm over your head and a pillow or folded towel under your left shoulder. This position flattens the breast and makes it easier to examine. Use the same circular motion described earlier. Repeat on your right breast.

The entire exam should take only a few minutes. Many women do a BSE before or after a shower, and go on to check their birthmarks, trim their toenails, or do other basic body care.

2

"No Problem" Breast Problems

At least once in your lifetime, you will probably notice something about your breasts that doesn't seem right. You might feel a lump that wasn't like this last month, or see a rash, or notice a discharge from your nipple or a puckering of the skin. This is one of the reasons it's a good idea to do regular breast self-exams, so you have an idea of what your breasts normally look and feel like. Then, if you do notice something that doesn't seem right, you can compare it to what you expected from your last BSE.

You may panic or immediately begin to deny the possibility of a problem with your health. Either way, you may feel uncomfortable, frightened, and confused. However, it may be reassuring to know that most women experience such breast scares, and for most of us, it turns out that there is nothing to worry about. But just to make certain there is no problem, it's always a good idea to see a doctor.

Your "Normal" Breasts

The main function of the mammary glands, or a woman's breasts, is to produce milk for newborns.

According to biologists, a "normal" female breast is one that can produce breast milk. All mammals have mammary glands, which enables females to breast-feed their babies. Human females have two mammary glands. Large or small, even or uneven, as long as a set of breasts produces milk for a newborn baby, they are regarded as medically normal.

Some men or boys develop firm breast tissue around or below one or both nipples. This is called gynecomastia, and it is usually due to hormone changes or, more rarely, to prescription drugs or illegal drugs. As many as 65 percent of fourteen-year-old boys have gynecomastia. This is not harmful, usually needs no treatment, and usually goes away within two to three years. A doctor will determine if a male has gynecomastia or simply has fat on his chest, which can be reduced by diet and exercise.

Breast Variations

There are many variations within the definition of "normal." One common variation is the extra nipple—an evolutionary leftover from the days when humans were more like other mammals who

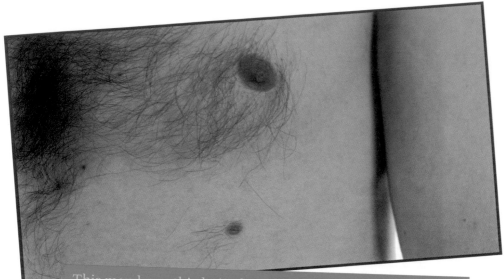

This man has a third nipple, called a supernumerary nipple, on his chest. According to a Wisconsin study in 2005, about 1 percent of Americans have an extra nipple or pair of nipples, and supernumerary nipples are slightly more common in males than in females.

often have multiple pairs of nipples. A little extra nipple may look more like a mole or birthmark. A few women actually have extra breast tissue, without a nipple, typically located under the armpit. Unless these "extras" cause physical discomfort or distress, there is no need to have them surgically removed. Men also can have an extra nipple or breast tissue, though in most men there is very little breast tissue at all.

Another normal variation is the diverse sizes of breasts, which is often hereditary. "Large" is a subjective term, however, because many women are comfortable with a size 36C, while others, especially petite females, might feel burdened and/or inhibited.

Real-life breasts come in a wide variety of shapes and sizes. Many lingerie stores provide an assortment of bra styles for comfort and support. You also could look at lingerie manufacturers on the Internet to find accessible options for purchasing bras.

The opposite variation is equally as subjective because being flat-chested or small-breasted can depend on both the opinion of the observer and the cultural values of the era. During the 1920s, for example, the fashion of the times dictated that it was attractive to be as flat-chested as a male, prompting women to bind their chests. There is a wide range of breast sizes and shapes, as well as a diverse range in bra sizes. Whether a bra is sized as small, medium, large, or from AA (the smallest cup size) to EE (the largest cup size), it is made to fit your chest size and your breasts so that it will be comfortable and offer your breasts the appropriate support.

These days, surgically enhanced breasts are "in," which has led to a boom in the business of cosmetic surgery. This surgery for breast enlargement has no medical benefit. There also is breast reduction surgery, done to reduce the size of very large breasts. For some women, young or old, breast reduction surgery is needed to improve posture and alleviate back pain. If done properly, breast surgery will not harm a woman's ability to nurse a child.

Some women have permanently inverted nipples, which are nipples that have grown inward instead of outward. This is not harmful. A simple surgical procedure can reverse this condition, but the results of surgery can prove to be merely temporary, with the nipples spontaneously returning to their inverted position. Some women with inverted nipples are able to nurse their babies without problems, and others may use a nipple shield to make the nipple stand out for easier suckling.

Despite the many variations, it is important to accept your breasts the way they are. After all, they are a part of you. If you are the least bit worried, you could talk to someone you trust, such as your mother or a doctor, about your concerns.

Breast Behavior

As you near or enter your teens, you will come up against the typically challenging life-cycle stage known as puberty. Hair begins to appear in your armpits and pubic area, your menstrual period starts, and your breasts begin to grow. Chemical messengers in the body, called hormones, trigger these steps toward sexual maturity.

For women, there is a cycle of hormones that usually takes around twenty-eight days. During this cycle, the ovaries release an egg cell and hormones to prepare her body in case she becomes pregnant. These hormones affect breast tissue, the uterus, and other parts of the body as well.

For females, the hormones estrogen and progesterone are most influential. As the levels of these hormones in the body naturally increase and begin to fluctuate, obvious physical and emotional changes occur. Sometimes you might feel moody, which could make you feel alternately cranky and on top of the world. You also will experience changes in your breast size and texture.

By learning to recognize the regularity of these physical and psychological changes, you'll begin to understand your body's cycles. Once you see the pattern—and understand that it is normal and healthy—you may feel more comfortable with your ever-changing body and psyche. You can use the chart below to tune in to the typical pattern for monthly breast changes as you begin to recognize your own special cycle.

When: During or just after your period (days 1–7).
What: Your breasts are full, tender, and sore but begin to return to normal by day 3 or 4.
Why: The hormones that started your period are shutting down.

When: Post-period (days 8–14).
What: Your breasts are normal, no swelling or soreness.
Why: The hormones are low.

When: Mid-cycle (days 15–20).
What: Your breasts begin to get fuller and more sensitive.
Why: The hormones are revving up again.

When: Just before your period (days 21–28).
What: Your breasts get more swollen, sore, and possibly lumpy.
Why: Hormones are high, starting up your period once again.

Lumps and Bumps

You'll be relieved to know that tender, lumpy breasts are normal at certain times of the month. But what if your breasts feel especially lumpy? Or what if, when you squeeze your nipples, some fluid oozes out? Or suddenly there's a big bump on one breast that feels either extremely hard or squishy? Are these the symptoms of breast cancer?

As a teenager, it is very unlikely that any lumps or bumps will turn out to be cancerous. But if you find something unusual in your breast, don't hesitate to make an appointment with your doctor for reassurance. There are other reasons besides cancer for lumps, and lumps should be understood, not ignored.

Normal lumpiness is due to the different types of tissue that make up your breasts. The milk-producing glands, structural tissue, and fat each have a different texture. Normal lumpiness feels like bunches of thickened tissue, not like a separate and distinct bump, which is usually something other than breast tissue. During your monthly cycle of hormones, some of these tissues may temporarily feel swollen or harder. Part of the reason for doing regular breast self-exams is to become familiar with the normal textures of your breasts.

If your doctor informs you that your lumpy breasts are due to fibrocystic disease or cystic mastitis, don't get nervous. These terms are actually old-fashioned labels that merely indicate your

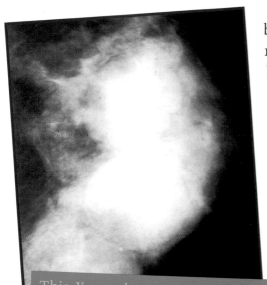

This X-ray shows a common non-cancerous breast condition called fibroadenoma. Fibroadenoma is characterized by the growth of fibrous tissues, cysts, inflammation, or infection in the breasts. This condition commonly affects women between the ages of thirty and fifty.

breast lumps are normal and noncancerous. "Fibrocystic breasts" means "normal breasts with normal lumps"—it refers to the fibrous tissues of the breast and cysts, which are lumps that are not harmful. This kind of lump will usually feel like ordinary breast tissue, but harder, and it gradually grows softer or smaller over a few weeks. Some women believe this lumpiness is a little more likely if you have bumped or bruised your breast, or have become sexually active. Most treatments for the lumpiness are ineffective, but many women do achieve relief by reducing or eliminating their intake of caffeine. If your lumps bother you, try cutting back on or cutting out all caffeinated products, such as coffee, tea, colas, and chocolate. If your lumps don't bother you, there is no need to treat them. You may prefer to wear a comfortable bra. Try various kinds, including sports bras, to see what feels best for you.

Some women experience breast pain, with or without lumps. This, too, is normal, but it can be annoying. Although no treatment has proven to be effective, reducing the extra fat in your diet may make a difference. This means cutting down on red meats, fried foods, fast foods, and rich desserts. Comfortable clothing may make a difference, so wear a well-fitting bra instead of one that is too tight or too loose. As well, some breast pains may actually be caused by a pulled muscle that attaches to your chest wall, between your breast and your rib cage. If this is the case, your doctor will help you plan how to avoid pulled muscle attachments in the future, usually by moderate exercise to promote strength after this pulled muscle heals.

Less Common Conditions

Breast infections, rashes, and nipple discharge are less common problems. These conditions need to be checked by your doctor. But rest assured, breast infections and discharges do not cause cancer.

If you have a rash on your breast or nipple, or a hot, swollen breast, tell your doctor. Most rashes are a simple reaction to friction from your clothing or perhaps an allergic reaction to deodorant or antiperspirant or laundry soap on your clothes. Friction from your clothing can cause a rash or rub your nipples raw. This is more likely if you are active in sports, jogging, or going on long runs, and it is often called "runner's nipple." It can affect both females and males. Most people find relief from washing with plain water and covering the nipples with a Band-Aid or Vaseline before the next sports activity. Wearing a sports bra is recommended while you are participating in a sport.

Some rashes are caused by eczema, psoriasis, and other skin conditions. There is a rare cancer called Paget's disease that makes a crusty rash and discharge on a nipple. Fewer than 2 percent of breast tumors are from Paget's disease, and both females and males can have it. Your doctor will be able to tell

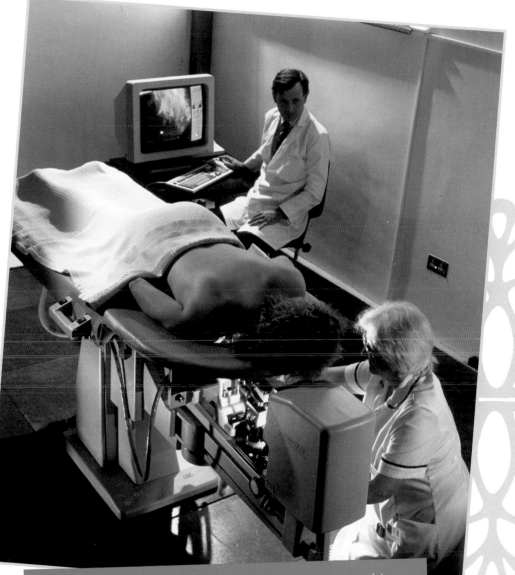

A woman who has a breast lump is undergoing a biopsy. The doctor and medical technician are using a digital X-ray camera and a needle that is being guided by a computer to obtain a tissue sample for testing.

10 Questions About Breast Problems

1 Does this problem with my breast mean I've got cancer and I'm going to die soon?

2 I'm really upset about this. Is there someone I can talk to about this?

3 Can my friend or mother accompany me in the examination room?

4 Is there something you can give me to read later?

5 What do you recommend that I do about this breast problem?

6 Is it important if I am (or think I might be) pregnant now?

7 Will this condition, or the treatment you recommend for it, affect my ability to become pregnant later?

8 Does this breast problem, or the treatment you recommend for it, affect my ability to be able to breast-feed?

9 Where can I learn more about this problem and possible treatments for it?

10 Is there a way to connect with others who are also experiencing this problem?

if your rash or discharge is anything to worry about, and what to do for it. Steroid cream will improve rashes caused by eczema or psoriasis, for example, but it will not improve a rash from Paget's disease.

If you ever discover a smooth, round, hard lump in one of your breasts, don't panic. Chances are the lump is a fibroadenoma, or noncancerous tumor. Teenagers are prone to developing harmless lumps, which can be the size of a pea or a marble. Even males can develop these lumps. Your doctor usually can tell just by feeling the growth if it is a fibroadenoma, which will move around freely in the breast tissue. He or she may recommend that your fibroadenoma be surgically removed, primarily so you won't keep worrying about it.

Cysts are more common in women who are in their thirties, forties, and early fifties. These squishy or hard fluid-filled sacs typically appear overnight, which can be a pretty scary discovery. A doctor will use a needle to drain out the fluid, immediately collapsing the cyst. Most cysts are a harmless nuisance and, like fibroadenomas, do not increase the risk for cancer. Nonetheless, you should still have them checked out by a doctor.

The best advice doctors have about breast infections, nipple discharges, rashes, fibroadenomas, or cysts is twofold: do not panic, but bring the matter to your doctor's attention right away. The statistical risk for breast cancer is no higher for women who have any of these problems. Let your doctor help you learn if any lump is cancer or merely a cyst or fibroadenoma.

3

Breast Cancer: Diagnosis and Prevention

In America, breast cancer is the leading cause of cancer death in women ages fifteen to fifty-four. However, the widespread fear of getting breast cancer sometimes keeps people from obtaining medical care and going to their doctors for annual physicals. Fear of breast cancer even can affect men, though breast cancer is very rare in men because most males have very little breast tissue. Fewer than one in 100 men with cancer has breast cancer or Paget's disease. Only 1 to 2 percent of all breast cancers are diagnosed in men instead of women. But anyone could be afraid for his or her female relatives and friends as much as for himself or herself.

Even though it is quite reasonable to hope that you will never have to face a diagnosis of breast cancer, you should arm yourself with the important and useful facts. By being informed, you can be sure to avoid or overcome unnecessary anxiety regarding this widely misunderstood disease.

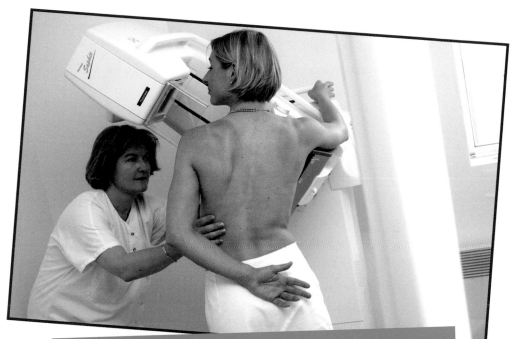

Doctors can screen for breast cancer by using mammography. Women usually begin getting mammograms after the age of thirty-five. Mammograms are not recommended for teens; if you detect an abnormal lump, your doctor can order an ultrasound to view the lump more closely.

A Doctor's Diagnosis

Breasts can have lumps for any of several reasons that have nothing to do with cancer. Only a doctor can diagnose whether or not a woman has breast cancer. Your responsibility is bringing any concerns you have to the doctor's attention and going for regular checkups as well as doing your BSE. A doctor may choose to do a biopsy or to aspirate (remove by suction) fluid from a cyst with a needle, or to remove a lump surgically and have it tested for cancer cells.

MYTH Breast cancer is the number-one killer of women in the United States.

FACT Heart disease kills ten times as many women as breast cancer does every year. More women die from lung cancer (primarily due to cigarette smoking) than breast cancer. Yes, the statistics do look bad—more than 110,000 American women were diagnosed with breast cancer in 2005. But that's fewer than the 175,000 who were diagnosed in 1996. With more than 140 million women and girls living in the United States, the percent of the total to be diagnosed with breast cancer is actually around 0.13 percent, or just over one-tenth of 1 percent per year.

MYTH Breast cancer is primarily a young woman's disease.

FACT The only factors proven to increase your risk for developing breast cancer are being a woman (men do get the disease, but very rarely) and aging. When you are under the age of twenty-five, your chances of getting the disease are less than one in 20,000. But as you grow older, your risk slowly increases, as it does for many other diseases, such as heart disease and diabetes.

MYTH If your mother or grandmother had breast cancer, you will probably get it, too.

FACT Around 80 percent of the women who are diagnosed with breast cancer do not have a mother, sister, or daughter with the disease. It is true that your risk increases if you have a close blood relative with breast cancer, but the vast majority of breast cancers arc not hereditary.

MYTH People who regularly eat right and exercise do not get cancer.

FACT Unfortunately, this is not always true. Good food and exercise reduce the risk but do not eliminate it. Although scientific studies indicate that certain life-style factors may reduce the chances for developing some cancers, including breast cancer, there are people who eat healthfully and participate in vigorous physical activity who do contract cancer.

Diagnosis by Mammograms

You may have heard of or read about the medical screening procedure called the mammogram. This is a photograph of your breasts made by special X-rays that detect very small breast lumps that cannot be felt by hand. As a teenager, a mammogram is not recommended. Young women's breast tissue is so dense that these X-rays are unable to reveal anything. You will probably not need a mammogram until you are thirty-five years old. If you have a family history of breast cancer, however, your doctor may urge you to get a mammogram earlier.

A mammogram is ordered by your doctor and done by a trained medical technologist. It takes only a few minutes to make an X-ray picture of first one breast, and then usually the other breast. The technologist will ask you if you are or might be pregnant, and if you think you are, he or she will place a lead apron over you to protect your ovaries from exposure to the X-rays. The X-ray machine has a ledge to place under your breast and a plastic brace to put over your breast. Some women find that their breasts are squeezed uncomfortably by the machine, but if you are hurting, tell the technologist at once. Technologists are trained to be as careful as possible.

Currently, women in their fifties are recommended to have a mammogram every two years, as part of basic cancer screening. By the time you are in your thirties or forties, however, there will probably be newer, more accurate screening tests and other proven preventive measures that will be recommended for breast health. With the successful advances that are expected for cancer research, treatment, and prevention over the next two decades, fewer women will have reason to fear the disease. With all that you know now, you can choose to be cautious and free of anxiety when it comes to the health of your breasts.

After Diagnosis

Medical researchers estimated in 2007 that more than 178,480 American women would be newly diagnosed with breast cancer. Most of these women have a very good chance of survival. Today, most women who are diagnosed with breast cancer and and are treated for it can expect to live at least five years—and many live a normal lifespan and eventually die not from breast cancer at all but from other natural causes instead.

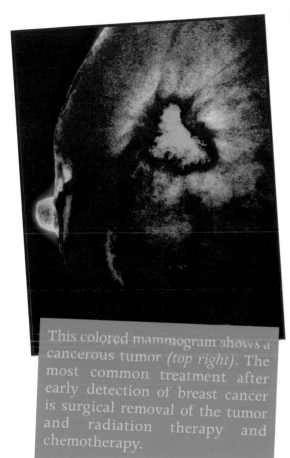

This colored mammogram shows a cancerous tumor *(top right)*. The most common treatment after early detection of breast cancer is surgical removal of the tumor and radiation therapy and chemotherapy.

In the United States, there are more than 250,000 women under the age of forty who are living with breast cancer. The five-year survival rate for young women with breast cancer is 82 percent, and for postmenopausal women, it is even higher.

There is no definite method to prevent breast cancer. However, by having a healthy lifestyle, including eating a well-balanced diet and exercising regularly, you can help lower your risk of developing certain cancers.

Prevention

There is no surefire way to prevent breast cancer. However, medical evidence supports a probable link between your behavior and your risk for certain cancers, such as breast cancer. This means you might want to make the lifestyle changes that scientists believe could make a difference in the long run. After all, living a healthy life can only help.

• **Eat a well-balanced diet.** Include lots of fresh, unprocessed fruits and vegetables, and eliminate processed foods, fried foods, red meat, and junk food (or keep your intake of them to a minimum). Avoid caffeine in coffee, tea, soft drinks, and chocolate.

- **Exercise.** Find physical activities you enjoy doing, then do them on a regular basis. Make exercise a fun part of your daily routine, even weekends and holidays.
- **Avoid becoming overweight.** No need to diet—just adopt the two suggestions above and you should naturally stay fit.
- **Take vitamin and mineral supplements.** Though some people prefer to take vitamin pills, and doctors do prescribe vitamin and mineral supplements for many pregnant women, most people will get all the vitamins and minerals they need from a well-balanced diet.
- **Avoid alcoholic beverages.** Some studies indicate there may be a link between drinking alcohol and an increased risk for breast cancer. Many studies have linked alcohol to a host of other diseases and problems as well.
- **Do not smoke cigarettes or other tobacco products.** Like alcohol, smoking cigarettes or other tobacco products has been linked to breast cancer.

Is Breast Cancer Hereditary?

One of the first things many people ask about cancer of any kind is if it is hereditary. Some women worry that because their mothers have breast cancer, they also will get it for sure. After all, if we inherit our eye color and our tallness and other things from our parents, would we also inherit cancer?

There are two answers to that question. The first is that we do not inherit cancer itself, but some people inherit genes that make it more likely to get certain kinds of cancer. The second answer is that some breast cancers, about a third of all diagnosed cases, seem to be genetically related. We can test for those mutant genes, some of which have been identified. Women who carry those genes can be particularly careful about making healthy lifestyle choices, doing regular BSEs, and having regular checkups with their doctors. Even if a woman has that same mutant gene as a close family member who has breast cancer, that does not guarantee she also will get breast cancer. It just means that the risk is higher for her than for the average woman.

More than three-quarters of all breast cancers are not related to these mutant genes. There is no one simple answer for why any one woman has breast cancer. It's probably for several reasons, some of which are inherited and some due to her life experiences, such as good or bad nutrition or exposure to industrial pollution.

Living with Fear

Many women who have lost their mothers or close relatives to breast cancer are fearful that they, too, will contract the disease. Rosie O'Donnell has been admirably candid in discussing her mother, who died of breast cancer when the popular comedienne and TV talk-show host was a child. As O'Donnell, who advocates breast health education, explains in her irreverently honest and straight-to-the-funny-bone style, "It seems plain that the more we know, the better equipped we will be to live life together with our boobs instead of in fear of them."

Colombian-American singer Soraya was deeply affected when her mother, grandmother, and a maternal aunt died of breast cancer. This encouraged her to inform Hispanic women about the disease. Soraya joined the Susan G. Komen Breast Cancer

This mother and daughter have breast cancer. The mother is undergoing chemotherapy, and the daughter, who is pregnant, had a mastectomy (removal of part or all of the breast) and will receive chemotherapy after her baby is born. The survival rate for both of these women is very high.

Foundation and traveled all over Latin America to educate women about early breast cancer detection. One of the songs recorded by this Latin Grammy–winning artist was based on her own experiences after she was found to have breast cancer in 2000. Before she died in May 2006, she wrote a letter in Spanish to her fans and posted it on her Web site. "I have not lost this battle, because I know the fight was not in vain," she said. "Instead, it will help end a larger battle, which is early detection to prevent this terrible disease."

4

Breast Implants: Boost or Bust?

Cosmetic surgery offers women with small breasts the chance to have their breasts appear larger. This surgery can be done after a mastectomy (the surgical removal of a breast) to restore the appearance of a breast. The majority of breast implants are not done for this reason, but rather as a cosmetic choice to make a woman's breasts appear larger.

Performers in the Public Eye

In October 1999, pop singer Britney Spears felt compelled to make a public announcement about the size of her breasts. To combat the rumors that surgical implants were behind her noticeably bigger bustline, the seventeen-year-old celebrity revealed the truth. It was a growth spurt—so common in girls her age—along with a twenty-five-pound weight gain. "In some interviews I

In 1999, seventeen-year-old singer Britney Spears made a public announcement about the size of her breasts to dispel rumors that she had undergone breast enlargement surgery. She explained that she had a sudden growth spurt and had gained weight.

would just start crying," the young superstar said in a newspaper article about the gossip focusing on her breasts. "I'd be like, 'Why are you being so rude to me?'"

Conforming to the standards of beauty valued in one's culture can be difficult and uncomfortable, even painful or unhealthy. And because the cultural ideals for feminine beauty typically are different from what is normal and common, many women, in seeking to attain these standards, often undermine their own sense of self-worth by changing their bodies.

Double Trouble

Many women who opt for surgical enhancement instead of self-acceptance end up regretting their choice. Yet the use of breast implants is still going on, despite a great deal of negative press about complications.

According to the American Society of Plastic and Reconstructive Surgeons, the number of breast-implant operations more than doubled between 1992 and 1996, with an estimated 90,000 women receiving surgically enlarged breasts in 1996 alone. In 2004, more than 264,000 breast augmentation procedures were performed. Complications from the surgery—in which synthetic baggies made from silicone and filled with saline, or saltwater, are inserted under or over the chest muscles—include infection, bleeding, deflation, and hardening of the scar tissue. Sometimes the implants leak, which some health experts and many women believe to be dangerous to health. Mammograms can prove difficult to read and interpret after one has had breast implants, which can result in the failure to detect cancer.

Top: A silicone breast implant *(left)* and a saline breast implant *(right)* are compared here. Bottom: A doctor holds a ruptured silicone implant *(center)* during a protest against the lifting of silicone implant restrictions.

In 1992, the U.S. government banned the use of silicone gel filler in breast implants (although the baggies are still made from it) because of the huge number of complaints that it caused a variety of health problems. So far, scientific studies have failed to prove the existence of a link between silicone in the body and the various illnesses some women experience after receiving breast implants. But the risks associated with this type of surgery are obvious. And the benefits are questionable.

5

Breast Health Instead of Fear

Because you are aware that the chances of being diagnosed with breast cancer at your age are pretty slim, you may feel less fearful of the disease. However, this does not mean that you should ignore the need to make healthy life choices now. Scientific studies indicate that successful prevention of breast cancer may begin very early in life. The choices you make today affect the health of your breasts in the future. And because the lifestyle factors that appear to best protect your breasts from disease are also good for your health in general, it makes sense to opt for the healthy choices now. By the time you are old enough to be at some risk for breast cancer, healthful living will be a natural part of your life.

These choices for a healthy lifestyle will not guarantee everyone a long life free from breast cancer. But they will lower the number of people who get any kind of cancer, including breast cancer. These choices will promote general good health, so people

In 2005, breast cancer survivors stand in the shape of a ribbon at the Susan G. Komen Breast Cancer Foundation Race for the Cure in Tyler, Texas. You can make a difference in your life and others' by organizing fun runs or walkathons to help raise money for breast cancer research and treatment.

are less likely to suffer from other health problems or injuries. And even if people who make healthy lifestyle choices do get cancer or have an accidental injury, the people are much more likely to have a prompt and complete recovery. Eating a well-balanced diet, exercising, avoiding being overweight, avoiding alcoholic beverages, and not smoking cigarettes or other tobacco products will help you remain healthy.

Positive Group Action

You are not the only woman—or person—to be taking an interest in breast health. Sometimes it feels right to get together with other people and do something positive that will make a difference in your lives and for others in your community. Most cities have walkathons and fun runs to raise money for breast cancer research and treatment. You could organize a fund-raiser to buy books on breast health for your local library, or volunteer at an event for La Leche League International, which supports mothers who breast-feed their babies. Being part of a group effort to promote breast health can be any of many things.

Individual and group efforts like these can come together to make each day a good day in itself. These efforts are part of a journey toward the future for which so many people hope, a time when all breast health problems can be remedied easily, without unnecessary fear or pain.

Glossary

areola Area around the nipple that appears darker than the rest of the breast.

benign Not cancerous.

biopsy Removal of tissue, surgically or with a needle, for testing purposes.

cancer Abnormal cell growth resulting in a variety of diseases.

cyst Fluid-filled sac.

estrogen Female sex hormone produced in varying amounts throughout the reproductive cycle.

fibroadenoma Benign tumor of the breast common in young women.

fibrocystic Outdated term used for lumpy breasts; merely indicates lumps are benign.

hormone Chemicals, produced by glands in the body, that travel through the bloodstream and influence various body tissues and functions.

mammary glands Glands in the breasts that, in females, produce and secrete milk.

mastectomy Surgery to remove the breast(s) and some of the surrounding tissue.

progesterone Female hormone involved in the menstrual cycle.

puberty The stage during physical and sexual maturation when the body becomes capable of reproduction.

silicone Synthetic material used in breast implants.

For More Information

Helping Children Cope Program Cancer Care, Inc.
275 7th Avenue
New York, NY 10001
(800) 813-HOPE
Web site: www.cancercare.org

> A national nonprofit organization that provides free, professional support services for anyone affected by cancer—patient, family/friend, or health care worker.

Just for Teens Y-Me National Breast Cancer Organization
212 West Van Buren
Chicago, IL 60607–3907
(800) 221-2141
Web site: www.y-me.org

> This organization focuses entirely on breast cancer and health, and provides information that's appropriate for teens' experience and reading level without talking down or oversimplifying content. It emphasizes quality of life and lifestyle improvement.

National Women's Health Information Center
A Project of the Office on Women's Health, U.S. Department of
    Health and Human Services
200 Independence Avenue SW, Room 730B
Washington, DC 20201
(800) 994-WOMAN

Web site: www.4woman.gov

  A U.S. government source for women's health information. The organization provides statistics and FAQs on information concerning breast health and issues related to health for girls and women.

The Susan G. Komen Breast Cancer Foundation
5005 LBJ Freeway, Suite 370
Dallas, TX 75244
(800) 462-9273
Web site: www.breastcancerinfo.com

  This foundation funds research grants and supports education, screening, and treatment projects in communities worldwide.

Web Sites

Due to the changing nature of Internet links, Rosen Publishing has developed an online list of Web sites related to the subject of this book. This site is updated regularly. Please use this link to access the list:

http://www.rosenlinks.com/gh/bcpr

For Further Reading

Albert, Louise. *Less Than Perfect*. New York, NY: Holiday House, 2004.

Boston Women's Health Collective. *Our Bodies, Ourselves: A New Edition for a New Era*. New York, NY: Touchstone/Simon & Schuster, 2005.

Davidson, James. *In Touch with Your Breasts: The Answers to Women's Questions About Breast Care*. Waco, TX: WRS Group, 2000.

Grover, Lorie Ann. *Loose Threads*. New York, NY: Simon & Schuster/Margaret K. McElderry, 2002.

Love, Susan, and Karen Lindsey. *Dr. Susan Love's Breast Book*. Reading, MA: Addison-Wesley, 2005.

Mohrbacher, Nancy, and Kathleen Kendall-Tackett *Breastfeeding Made Simple: Seven Natural Laws for Nursing Mothers*. Oakland, CA: New Harbinger Publications, 2005.

Murphy, Beth. *Fighting for Our Future: How Young Women Find Strength, Hope and Courage While Taking Control of Breast Cancer*. New York, NY: McGraw-Hill, 2003.

O'Donnell, Rosie, and Deborah Axelrod. *Bosom Buddies: Lessons and Laughter on Breast Health and Cancer*. New York, NY: Warner Books, 1999.

Smith, Terry L. *Breast Cancer: Current and Emerging Trends in Detection and Treatment*. New York, NY: The Rosen Publishing Group, 2006.

Waters, Sophie. *Seeing the Gynecologist*. (Girls' Health). New York, NY: Rosen Publishing, 2007.

Bibliography

American Cancer Society. *Breast Cancer Facts & Figures 2005–2006*. Atlanta, GA: American Cancer Society, Inc., 2005.

Ben-Joseph, Elana Pearl. "Why Are My Breasts Different Sizes?" KidsHealth.org. August 2004. Retrieved June 9, 2006 (http://www.kidshealth.org/teenquestion/just_girls/breast_size.html).

"Breast Cancer." MayoClinic.com. July 14, 2006. Retrieved October 27, 2006 (http://www.mayoclinic.com/health/breast-cancer/DS00328).

"Breast Problems in Men." FamilyDoctor.org. Retrieved January 29, 2007 (http://familydoctor.org/520.xml).

"Gynecomastia: When Breasts Form in Males." FamilyDoctor.org. Updated December 2006. Retrieved January 29, 2007 (http://familydoctor.org/080.xml).

Murphy, Beth. *Fighting for Our Future: How Young Women Find Strength, Hope and Courage While Taking Control of Breast Cancer*. New York, NY: McGraw-Hill, 2003.

National Cancer Institute. "Breast Cancer." Retrieved January 29, 2007 (http://www.cancer.gov/cancertopics/types/breast).

O'Donnell, Rosie, and Deborah Axelrod. *Bosom Buddies: Lessons and Laughter on Breast Health and Cancer*. New York, NY: Warner Books, 1999.

Smith, Terry L. *Breast Cancer: Current and Emerging Trends in Detection and Treatment*. New York, NY: Rosen Publishing Group, 2006.

Index

Photo Credits

Cover, pp. 1, 3, 4, 22 © www.istockphoto.com; p. 6 © www.istockphoto.com/ blaney photo; p. 8 © www.istockphoto.com/Phil Date; p. 13 © www.istock photo.com/Iskra Marinova; p. 14 © Custom Medical Stock Photo; p. 15 © China Photos/Getty Images; p. 19 © T. Youseff/Custom Medical Stock Photo; p. 21 © Geoff Tompkinson/Photo Researchers, Inc.; p. 25 © Phanie/Photo Researchers, Inc.; p. 29 © Zephyr/Photo Researchers, Inc.; p. 30 © www. istockphoto.com/mandygodbehear; p. 33 © Sonda Dawes/The Image Works; p. 36 © Dave Hogan/Getty Images; p. 38 *(top)* © Spencer Platt/Getty Images; p. 38 *(bottom)* © Frazer Harrison/Getty Images; p. 40 © AP/Wide World Photos.

Designer: Evelyn Horovicz; **Editor:** Kathy Campbell
Photo Research: Amy Feinberg